MW00425952

How the Paper Fish
Learned to Swim

Dear Todd,

Your kindness and
encouragement mean
so much to me.

Peace,

Jonathan

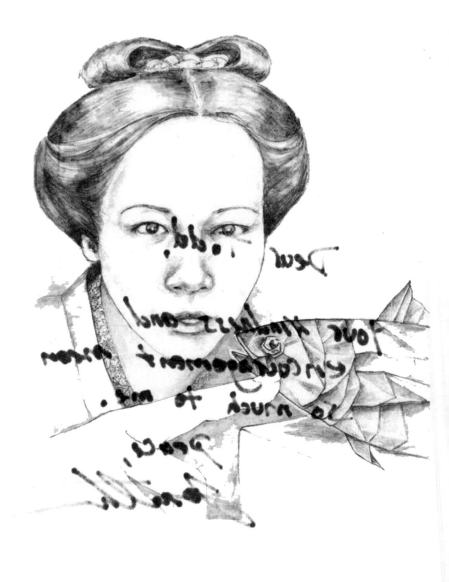

How the Paper Fish Learned to Swim

A Fable About Inspiring Creativity

and Bringing New Ideas to Life

JONATHON A. FLAUM
ILLUSTRATIONS BY RAINA BAYS

AMACOM

AMERICAN MANAGEMENT ASSOCIATION
New York • Atlanta • Brussels • Chicago • Mexico City • San Francisco
Shanghai • Tokyo • Toronto • Washington, D.C.

Special discounts on bulk quantities of AMACOM books are
available to corporations, professional associations, and other
organizations. For details, contact Special Sales Department,
AMACOM, a division of American Management Association,
1601 Broadway, New York, NY 10019.
Tel.: 212-903-8316. Fax: 212-903-8083.
Website: www.amacombooks.org

This publication is designed to provide accurate and authoritative
information in regard to the subject matter covered. It is sold with
the understanding that the publisher is not engaged in rendering
legal, accounting, or other professional service. If legal advice or other
expert assistance is required, the services of a competent professional
person should be sought.

Library of Congress Cataloging-in-Publication Data

Flaum, Jonathon A., 1968–
        How the paper fish learned to swim : a fable about inspiring creativity and
bringing new ideas to life / Jonathon A. Flaum ; illustrations by Raina Bays.
        p.   cm.
    Includes index.
    ISBN-10: 0-8144-0888-5 (hardcover)
    ISBN-13: 978-0-8144-0888-9 (hardcover)
    1. Creative ability in business.   2. Leadership.   I. Title.

    HD53.F635   2007
    658.4'063—dc22   2006012217

Printing number

10   9   8   7   6   5   4   3   2   1

For Tami. My wife and best friend.

"*There is nothing with which every man is so afraid as getting to know how enormously much he is capable of doing and becoming.*" —SOREN KIERKEGAARD

"It is our duty as men and women to proceed as though the limits of our abilities do not exist."

—PIERRE TEILHARD DE CHARDIN

Contents

Contents

Acknowledgments

The tale in this book was originally inspired by a three-dimensional paper fish created by artist Charlie Th'ng. The fish felt so lifelike that I couldn't help but think it wanted to go to the ocean.

A debt of gratitude is owed to all the practitioners who come to the Zen Center of Asheville, or Daishinji, as we call it. For the character of "Daishinji" I imagined this physical space of openness coming to life. I particularly want to thank Rev. Teijo Munnich, Art Mandler, Randal Pride, Marcus Chatfield, Paige Gilchrist, Jenny Knapp, Debra Barlow, and Al Kopf, for their presence and encouragement at Zen Center these years.

My mom, Susan Kastin, read an early version of the manuscript; made some helpful suggestions; and, as always, was a voice of kindness. My dad, Sander Flaum, coauthor on my first book, has been a cheerleader and friend on this. The same goes for my stepdad, Joel Kastin, and my stepmom, Mechele Flaum, who never seem to run out of words of encouragement. And I want to acknowledge my sister, Pamela Weinberg, who continues to amaze me with her competence and compassion.

I want to thank Raina Bays, for her insight and care in bringing the story to life with her pictures; Erika Spelman, for her astute copyediting; and my editor at AMACOM, Adrienne Hickey, for being such a genuine advocate, honest critic, and teacher.

Neither this book, nor anything of much consequence in my life, would be possible without my wife, Tami, so I thank her as always. I thank my children too: my son, Ren, whose imagination inspires my own, and my daughter, Eve, who reminds me that holding a baby is the thing that takes precedence over all else in this world.

Part I

THE FABLE

About 500 years ago there was a young origami master named Daishinji who lived in a small fishing village in Japan.

Daishinji was beginning to become well known for what she could do with a single sheet of paper.

One day she decided to fold a sheet of paper into a fish.

Daishinji was amazed by it; she thought it to be a masterpiece and so did others.

Daishinji

The fish was fully shaped. With its folds of fins and gills, it looked almost real.

One day, after listening for a long time, the paper fish finally spoke.

The Paper Fish Speaks

His first three words were: "I am lonely."

Pleased by the fish's ability to communicate, Daishinji said, "Then I'll fold you a world in which to swim."

And so an entire folded world was made from paper—an ocean, seaweed, swordfish, whales, sharks, lobsters, crabs, an octopus, and even birds above.

For a long time this was good, and the paper fish was happy.

But then one day the paper fish realized that as deep as he swam he would never get wet.

And this seemed odd to him, to be a fish, but not to feel the wetness of water.

The paper fish begged to go to the real ocean, which was deep, wet, and full of mysteries unknown to Daishinji.

The young master began to get frustrated. After all, she had spent months building a world for her paper fish. "Imaginary things must stay in imaginary places," Daishinji shouted with an anger that the paper fish did not recognize.

The paper fish would not take "No" for an answer. His determination was like that of a samurai, and Daishinji finally relented.

Although she knew in her heart that paper was only paper, Daishinji agreed to take the paper fish out to the deep, black, real ocean.

So the next morning as the sun was rising, the young origami master placed the paper fish in a red wooden box and secured it to her father's fishing boat.

Into the Boat

Daishinji steered the boat to the center
of the sea, far away from the small studio
that was so comfortable to her.

Out to Sea

The paper fish was safe and dry in the waterproof box, but he became increasingly excited as he felt the pulse of the waves swell under the boat.

Finally, after what felt like forever to the paper fish, the master stopped the boat, dropped anchor, and lifted her creation out of the walls of the red box.

"See the rough, rolling sea?" shouted Daishinji above the crashing waves rocking the boat. "Is this what you want?"

"I want the real sea!" the paper fish shouted back.

"Trust enough to place me in it and I will become as real and full of blood and bones as any fish swimming at the greatest depths."

The young origami master decided that her paper fish needed to learn a lesson.

Daishinji lifted her folded creation, placed him on top of the ocean, and let go for just an instant, figuring that as the paper got wet and began to disintegrate, the fish would scream to be brought back onto the boat.

But no such thing occurred.

In the instant that Daishinji let go of the paper fish an amazing transformation took place. If Daishinji had not seen it with her own eyes, she would not have believed it.

Paper turned to flesh and folds turned to fins and gills.

The blood rushing into his body was as fire burning paper away.

The fish let out an anguished scream as if he were dying, but then the cry became one of joy.

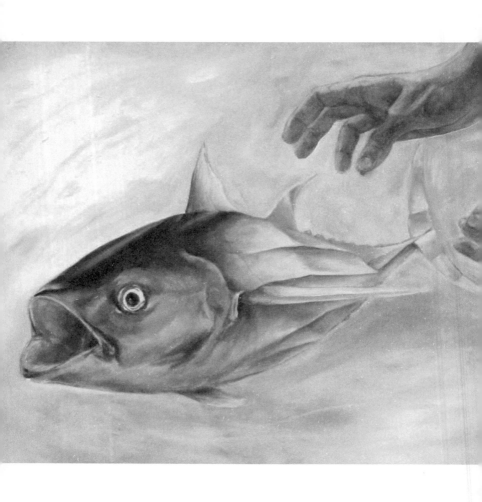

The Fish Becomes Real

Daishinji gasped and then held a great breath as the paper she had folded with her hands in her private studio transformed before her eyes into a giant, radiant yellowtailed tuna.

The yellowtailed fish did not look back at Daishinji once he hit the real ocean. He simply swam on into the deep.

"One day you may get caught in a net, now that you are real. My father may bring you back to market so you can be supper for the village!" Daishinji screamed anxiously.

The wide-eyed finned giant finally turned back and shouted, "But now I am free—as real as you are!"

Goodbye

And then the yellowtail splashed a spray of water to the sky and swam down deeper than any fish had ever gone.

Daishinji finally released her anxiety and began sobbing.

The ocean rocked her from below like her mother once had.

After what felt like a lifetime, silence returned.

A tender smile of renunciation appeared on Daishinji's lips.

"I don't even know your name . . ." she whispered to the emptiness.

Daishinji focused on the vast sea and on the empty red box until the two became one to her.

When the time seemed right, she pulled up her anchor and turned her boat for home.

After many years of folding paper, Daishinji became known all over Japan as a great master.

$\mathcal{S}$he created worlds on paper that all became real in their own time.

One day, a young origami practitioner sought out Daishinji. She asked the old woman why she bothered to make things if she then just let them go, holding on to nothing to show for her labor.

A Young Visitor

Daishinji thought a while.

She looked around her shop until she
found the old dusty box with just speckles
of red paint remaining on it.

Daishinji asked the young apprentice if she had come by boat. The apprentice said she had, and Daishinji suggested that they take a ride together. She instructed the young woman to drop anchor when they got to the center of the ocean.

Daishinji then told the apprentice to go to the side of the boat with the worn wooden box and bid a fish to jump in so they could look at it.

The apprentice went to the side of the boat and did as Daishinji instructed her.

Nothing happened for a time.

Then, out of nowhere, the largest yellowtailed tuna the apprentice had ever seen jumped into the boat.

The Giant Tuna Jumps

The force of it knocked Daishinji and the apprentice overboard.

Daishinji was laughing hard as her old friend, the onetime paper fish, got hold of her and the apprentice and helped them back onto the boat.

The apprentice watched as the onetime paper fish told his creator, "There is no going back."

"There Is No Going Back"

"I know," said Daishinji. And she pulled up the anchor and instructed the origami apprentice to steer back to shore.

The young woman and the old one were silent on the ride back.

When they reached shore, the apprentice implored Daishinji, "Master, will you please teach me what you know?"

"I just did," said Daishinji.

The Master

Part II

FROM FABLE
INTO PRACTICE

What is there to learn from the story of Daishinji and the paper fish that will apply to your work as a manager or team leader? This section of the book is meant to help you translate the teachings of the fable into effective ways of nourishing creativity and innovation in your team—and in yourself. It will help you become a "Daishinji manager."

An Introduction

When Daishinji is young and brazen and full of the delight of her own power as a creator, she feels angry at the paper fish for having the audacity to want to live in the real world. In a fit of rage, she screams, "Imaginary things must stay in imaginary places!" Up to this point, the paper fish had experienced his creator as kind, inspired, and open. But as soon as Daishinji is challenged to let go of her creation and let it live free in the world, she digs in her heels. To cross from imagination to reality seems like an unbridgeable gap. But the young Daishinji is wrong. The way Daishinji changed from the time she was a young hot shot to the time she became known as an old master is instructive for managers who want to transform their status-quo culture into an innovation culture.

Einstein proclaimed that "imagination is more powerful than knowledge," and he was right. We can know absolutely everything about the past through study and as much as we can about the present through constant analysis, but the future will always remain a mystery. We can only imagine the future. This is what every great inventor and intellectual pioneer dared to do. These innovators had the audacity to believe the opposite of the young Daishinji—they proclaimed that imaginary things do indeed have a place in the real world. And such an attitude seems possible when you think of the power of an individual mind—Cezanne or Beethoven or Marie Curie or even Einstein himself. But it gets more complicated in a group setting—let alone in one where the pressure of profit is part of the equation. But it can be done. An environment where creativity is fostered can be created right in the heart of a public company or small business that has a mandate to make a profit. But to do it we need the help of Daishinji.

We tend to think of great innovators in the singular—in business, people like Bill Gates, Steve Jobs, or Andy Grove come to mind. But the truth is that individuals like these are one in a million and could innovate out of their garage as easily as they could their corner office. The question for organizations has always been how to multiply the impact of great innovators—how to teach others to be innovative. This book is written for managers interested in teaching everyone on their team how to go through a creative process that produces innovative results. Individual innovative stars may start a new company or invent a great product, but an individual alone cannot carry the day over the long term. For a company to be innovative consistently over the long term, a creative management culture must be in place. Stars come and go, while a process embeds innovation as a way of working, not as a hoped-for happenstance. To best understand "Daishinji management," we have to understand how adhering methodically to a creative process can unleash innovation in any company.

Throughout this commentary I will refer to examples that involve mounting a theater production, producing a film, or creating a dance piece. I do this specifically because the arts have always been a place where creative collaboration is the key. A "manager" in the arts (director, designer, choreographer) evolves from a tradition of managing talent through a creative process that will lead to the development of an innovative product, for example, a show, a major motion picture, or a ballet. In business we have not yet discovered our own best practices to undertake the kind of intentional creative process that can produce an innovative result. The arts have had this figured out for a long time; we study them here to see how we can use this established wisdom to help business at a time when innovation, not administration, is the urgent demand.

Daishinji herself is a rather strange character. I met her almost seven years ago and for the longest time she didn't say a word to me . . . she wanted me to figure things out for myself. Her name translated into English means "magnanimous mind temple." And so on our road to creating a work space where creativity and innovation can thrive we will start by exploring what it means to create an atmosphere at work that is open and yet cared for and guarded with the respect one would give a "temple." Once we have a sense of how to create a magnanimous mind temple at work, we will go on to discuss five lessons that Daishinji taught me about the power of (1) Autonomy, (2) Letting Go, (3) Exchange, (4) Collaboration, and (5) Innovation. These lessons, when practiced with effort, can yield a space where people become who they need to be and discover that which was hidden from them before, thereby delivering unprecedented results in the workplace.

It is important to note that what is described here is not a single event. Employing this process implies that the company has undergone a cultural shift that demonstrates the value being placed on innovation. People must carry on their "day jobs" within the organization, including all administrative minutiae, but if time is not set aside daily, weekly, monthly, quarterly, and yearly for intentionally managed episodes designed to spur innovation, the company will soon have little left to administrate. In today's global business climate, it is breakthrough disruptive innovation that drives a company's bottom line. "More of the same" can no longer sustain a business. This is why the following process is meant to be integrated into a company's culture and not construed as an extracurricular activity to do on an outsourced basis once in a while.

It is also crucial to understand that everyone on the team can be creative. It is the supposition of this book that with the right atmosphere developed and preserved by the manager, everybody on the team can make creative contributions that lead to innovation at every level of the organization. In the current economy, this is not only possible, but necessary. There are fewer job functions that exist simply to maintain a business. More companies are looking at every position on their payroll as something that should add value to the growth of the organization. In this sense, each person on the payroll is expected to behave much more like an entrepreneur or consultant than a standard employee executing a limited task. Therefore, when a problem/challenge arises, the solution cannot be outsourced to a "creative shop" or "consultancy." The internal team is now charged with having the expertise and dynamism of a creative consultancy. And to do this, teams require a new style of management—one that understands the relationship between the execution of daily tasks and the need to create "pockets of time" to employ the creative process that leads to innovation.

Magnanimous Mind: Infinite Possibility in the Workplace

IN PRINCIPLE

The life of what we create is not separate from us. If we choose to shut down our creations, we shut down ourselves. It was only because Daishinji went the distance in listening to the demands of the paper fish that she went on to become a great master.

Sometimes we are under the illusion that ideas are ours to possess because they came into our mind, but this is a fallacy. Ideas are not ours. The reality is that we do not know where ideas come from. Do they come from dreams? Well then, where do dreams come from? We can't control how we get inspired or what inspires us any more than we can control our need to breathe. Such things are simply gifts. Creators are the mediators of inspiration; they are not the sources of it. This was a lesson that Daishinji needed to learn from the paper fish.

It takes humility to know that we don't control ideas; they just happen to us when we remain open to them. The key is to "listen" to what direction the idea has in mind. If we don't listen to an idea but instead rush to put it in a cage (or on a canvas, in a book, or in a business plan) and slap a price tag on it, we risk short-circuiting the creative process. We risk winding up with something that looked great on paper but that never had the chance to develop into something substantial enough to live under its own power in the world.

To work with a magnanimous mind is to trust a new idea more than you do the old notions of what is possible and what isn't—to follow Einstein's credo and trust in the imagination. To do such a thing requires having faith in the creative process; it also requires having the confidence to risk looking like a fool.

Consider the Wright Brothers. Imagine what the townsfolk of Dayton, Ohio, said about these two bachelor bicycle mechanics who swore they were going to fly. But Orville and Wilbur Wright followed the germ of their idea and went from their paper sketches to a real-life flying machine—no special education, no investor financing, just an idea that they were prepared to follow wherever it led them.

The paper fish teaches Daishinji that her work as an artist is not about creating objects but about giving life to what lives inside her. Watching things she creates take on life becomes more worthwhile to Daishinji than grasping at her creations and relegating them to mere transactions. This generosity of mind is the very thing that puts Daishinji on a path to mastery. There is no roadblock between inspiration and representation—no people in the way who want glory for themselves.

The apprentice who comes to Daishinji has not yet arrived in such a place—her self is in the way. She still sees the world in terms of what she can gain from it rather than what she can give to it. The young woman at first has no context for understanding Daishinji. She asks why Daishinji bothers to make things if she ends up letting them go. Daishinji does not answer the apprentice with words at first; she knows that an action that will alter the perceptive reality of the apprentice is the only way to teach her. And so they travel to the center of the ocean.

Daishinji shows the apprentice that in the center there is reason to observe with the curiosity of a child. With a sense of awe after meeting the fish of paper that became flesh the apprentice says: "Master, will you please teach me what you know?" How do we learn that our ideas are bigger than us and will outlive us if we can get out of their way? This is our work.

IN PRACTICE

As a manager how can you listen to ideas as though they are living entities? Ideas are "action-potentials"— capable of moving a company forward in a way that standard strategies are not geared to do. Innovative ideas excite a room, a market, and a customer base. To cultivate a magnanimous mind as a manager is to be open to the "borders" of the business. It is to be generous with what may feel like a creative person's play. A magnanimous mind is a free one not bent on making distinctions, but rather dedicated to finding connections for ideas that at first glance seem like just "something that looks good on paper."

Cultivation of magnanimous minds in the workplace is contagious. This means that as a manager you have to practice magnanimity yourself first. This practice entails not viewing yourself as a function at work, but instead as a full person who is of value specifically because of your idiosyncrasies. In a global marketplace where innovation, not rational production, is what makes or breaks a company, your uniqueness is your greatest asset. Fitting into a corporate mold is almost certain death for a person looking to thrive in the global competition for new ideas.

Competent functionality is not enough in business anymore—competent functionality is too easily outsourced at a rate at which you couldn't comfortably live in the United States or Europe or many parts of Asia. What is valuable about you in this new economy isn't what you learned in business school; it's what you didn't. The new imperative for survival is to fully be who you are—warts and all.

An innovative result demands an innovative atmosphere in which to create that result. The following chapters will focus in detail on how to create such an atmosphere for your creative team at work.

The hope is that by learning how to create an innovative atmosphere you actually become innovative and, in fact, magnanimous. No longer relegated to creating management systems that keep people in hierarchical reporting structures, you are now charged with developing an atmosphere conducive to producing interactions that spark innovation. Management has never been a more daring activity!

The "Paper Fish Process" begins with Daishinji or a "magnanimous mind temple." The manager is charged with creating an atmosphere geared to big open thinking rather than administrative efficiency. Not that the choice is a simple "either/or." You can have both administrative efficiency and the kind of creativity that leads to innovation, but you must be precise in how you arrange this balance. People must perform their daily functions, but if that is all they do, new ideas to grow the company will not magically appear.

As a manager, it is up to you to set the tone for innovation. The Paper Fish Process can be something that is scheduled monthly (for small issues), quarterly (for larger ones), and yearly (for the largest). The manager could also enact the Process at any time she feels it is necessary to get the group through a problem/issue that has arisen unexpectedly (e.g., a competitor's new product launch or business model). A call to enact the Process can also happen informally among team members who become comfortable with its structure and see a need to play it out.

For the Process to remain a living thing, you must

make a daily practice of it. Otherwise it is likely to be relegated to an outsourced event with no impact on day-to-day company culture.

To do this, there must be silence for the first fifteen minutes of each workday. Instituting this requires asking people to come in earlier. The phones must be on mute and alert systems off on any e-mails, electronic planners, and cell phones. For that early period of the day people are doing nothing but cultivating their magnanimous mind. They are charged with thinking big about the business and the team's role in it and recording those ideas as they develop in their "Daishinji Journal." Each Friday morning ideas are shared in a short Daishinji meeting run by the manager of the team. No judgments or evaluations are made at this time; it is just a brief sharing of ideas so people can inspire each other, meet if their ideas coincide, and learn from each other's progress. The manager's function is to ask questions and encourage; his direct reports are charged with going beyond surface change to disruptive innovation.

From one week to the next the manager can clearly see when it is time to call together a formal Paper Fish Process.

THE CASE

The fictitious case that we will examine throughout this commentary to help us understand how the Process works is a subsidiary of a large North American media conglomerate that owns over 200 newspapers and radio stations in a variety of markets. This particular daily newspaper, called the *Maple,* has been consistently losing market share for months. The multimedia conglomerate that acquired it some years ago has grown impatient with its progress. Unsentimental about anything but share price, the conglomerate has put the *Maple*'s publisher on notice that if the paper cannot become profitable again within the next year, it will be discarded. The publisher has already cut staff down to bare bones as the conglomerate advised. There is nothing left to cut; it is innovation that is the urgent demand.

The publisher, Mike Holloway, has run the paper for the last six years and watched profits dwindle steadily as competition from innovative local and national online news sites has taken bites out of his market share. With nowhere left to turn, he decides to employ the Paper Fish Process. He gathers together his managing editor, Rudy Vega; his advertising manager, Dean Moriarty; his longtime manager of the classified section,

Bella Naropa; and his young news editor, Andrea Molloy. Mike asks each of them to spend fifteen minutes of quiet every morning contemplating how profitability can happen not through more cost cutting but through the creation of a new business model. They all know that each of their jobs and those of their colleagues and charges depend on their creativity.

Autonomy: Allowing Creative Talent to "Be" at Work

IN PRINCIPLE

Daishinji's autonomy is crucial for her because it provides an atmosphere where she can interact with her creation, without interruption or distraction. Daishinji, in owning her creative power, learns to renounce her conscious desire to control the outcome of that power. To try to control it would have limited it. Creators need time alone with their creations. They need time to realize the power of transmitting something inside them into a reality outside them. They need time to realize that it didn't happen because they willed it, but rather because they got their will out of the way and allowed the creative idea to speak through them without interruption.

The great paradox of autonomy in the creative process is that in the end it must be renounced, but in the beginning no creative act is possible without it. For a creative idea to live in the world as an independent reality the creator needs to ultimately get out of the way. To do this with equanimity the creator first must have total control of the project and be free of bureaucratic interruption and outside criticism.

A way to understand this process is to see how it works in film. One of the greatest living film directors is Clint Eastwood. Actors report that the unique thing about working on a set with Eastwood is the quiet. Movie sets are usually notorious for their noise—all the rigging and cable being lugged around and all of the people doing their jobs off camera. It's why the phrase "quiet on the set" has been so indelibly marked on us. It is what we think directors do—quiet down the external noise so the actors can focus and the camera can pick up a real moment. But for Eastwood, the atmosphere is always quiet and the autonomy of actors is never impinged upon by reminders of commercial reality.

Eastwood sets this up for the actors and for himself as well; his sets offer a refuge for creative play and unconscious accident—a refuge for a script developed on paper to transform into a real world. Perhaps it helps that Eastwood is a musician and frequently scores his own films. In the reflective quiet he hears the rhythm of the piece, hears its flow and its spaces for silence. This is why watching movies Eastwood has directed is such a powerful experience, because in the actors' impeccable performances we discover not just the heart of a character, but our own heart as well. The creative autonomy Eastwood grants the actors somehow transfers to our own autonomy of feeling as a member of the audience.

In the end we see that though we think the creator creates the creation, it is actually the creation that creates the creator. People become what they were meant to be when they see what they can do in the world. They need autonomy to see such a vision of who they can be, and when they have it they do not simply create; they are created.

IN PRACTICE

The creative process does not always gel in a group at first go-round. Creative people need space and time. A walk, a bike ride, an hour in the garden, or even a half hour working with clay can unlock a complicated issue at work in a way that staring at a computer screen in an office or sitting at a meeting in a hotel conference room never could. The "first draft" of a thought or idea is often quite tentative—it comes to us intuitively. Over-analyzing it rationally right away (particularly in a group immediately intent on gauging the ROI) can kill a potentially great outcome. Creative people require the freedom to "dream it up" before they can be asked to "tie it down" to strategically executable plans. Teresa Amabile, Ph.D., the Edsel Bryant Ford Professor of Business Administration at Harvard Business School, who has studied creativity for over twenty years, said: "The most effective way to stifle creativity is to make people feel that they have no discretion or autonomy" ("Creativity on the Clock" in the American Psychological Association's *Monitor on Psychology,* Volume 34, No. 10, November 2003, p. 56). In this same article, the findings of psychologist Jung Zhou, Ph.D., of Rice University's Jones Graduate School of Management are also presented. Zhou found that "the presence of creative co-workers can foster employee innovation, but only when supervisors do not engage in close monitoring." Zhou defines "close monitoring" as "frequent and intrusive check-ups by supervisors."

The autonomy phase marks the official enactment

of the Paper Fish Process. Depending on the complexity of the problem the manager may provide team members with a half day, a full day, or, in some cases, up to a week of completely free autonomous time in which they are given a reprieve from their daily administrative duties and assignments and are free to pursue the creative process that leads to innovation.

The Daishinji manager trusts the people who work for her to the degree that she is prepared to let them be during the autonomous phase of the creative process. The Daishinji manager realizes that autonomy is not the only stage, but she also realizes that if the autonomous stage is rushed over or skipped, then the kind of innovation the company is looking for is impossible to achieve.

During this stage the manager is a protector of the creative process—the guardian of the team. The manager's job is to clearly describe the nature of the company's problem or aspiration. The manager must describe the market forces within the industry and within the global environment that are affecting this problem or aspiration. The manager should not be specific about the parameters of the solution. Rather, she should be as specific as possible when describing the issue and as vague and open ended as possible in discussing how one might go about resolving it.

During the autonomy period the employees' time is

their own to spend. If it works for them to come into the office every day, that is fine. If it works better for them to work out of a cabin an hour away, that too is fine. No limitation should be imposed except that when the allotted time is up each team member is expected to return to the office and make a full presentation of an idea that he or she has developed.

This might seem strange at first, to manage people by not managing them, but the kind of creativity that unleashes innovation is not amenable to being controlled. An environment can be set up for it to work—a great studio space for a painter or an interesting plot of ground for a landscape architect—but a result cannot be dictated. At this stage of the process a manager is more like a great patron than a boss. As the Medici family was to Michelangelo so is the manager to the team that is responsible for creating new value for the company.

A manager should be likened to a film director. A director selects an actor to play a part because he believes in the actor's ability to bring something to the role that the director never could have imagined on his own. In this new economy a core necessity of any manager is his ability to choose talent. As they say in film, "casting is 90 percent of the director's job." It is the same for a manager. When the manager selects well he can simply let these talented individuals do their jobs.

And in the autonomy stage this means protecting their creative space. In this phase a director gives the actor the script and says: "Create this character." The director may not see the actor again for some time, but when he does he will be confident that the actor returns to the set prepared with a fully formed character. Think of the preparation Robert De Niro put in to bring Jake LaMotta to life in *Raging Bull* or how Anthony Hopkins created Hannibal Lecter for *The Silence of the Lambs.* No director, no matter how good, could have dictated those performances. Those performances are remembered so many years later and will continue to be referenced in the annals of film history because the directors gave the performers the time to create the unexpected.

A Daishinji manager likewise tells her creative talent: "Here is the situation; now go and create its resolution. Show me what it looks like when I see you again." The talent is treated like a professional who has the power to transform. If, with this freedom, he or she cannot deliver, then that person will not continue to be "cast" in the future. No blame or ceremony, just a simple exit. Actors are cast again because of their ability to perform, not because of their seniority or political connections. A manager, by taking the same approach, winds up with a team of top performers. A manager never has to be reduced to coddling or scolding; she simply lets the performance speak for itself.

There will be time to make sure that the creative people under your charge have been accountable to you with regard to the assignment, but the autonomy phase is not that time. During this time the creative talent should feel that the only thing they are accountable to is the integrity of their ideas. The result is that the people reporting to you will love their work because in reporting to you they actually get a chance to report to their own creative process. And in this new economy of talent, where hierarchy and the drive for external prestige are quickly dying, there is no better way to secure employee loyalty.

THE CASE

In the case of the *Maple,* the publisher, Mike Holloway, has seen the writing on the wall for a long time. His newspaper has been losing readership and general and classified advertising revenue for some time. When the newspaper began eighty years ago there was no Internet, flash animation, or podcasts. And there weren't nearly as many combinations of news sources available from every corner of the world.

Mike pulls his team together and asks them to each

take a week alone to come up with an idea to save the newspaper. His staff includes Rudy Vega, the sixty-three-year-old managing editor who has been at the paper since the days when there was a morning and an evening edition; Andrea Molloy, the thirty-one-year-old news editor five years out of Northwestern; Dean Moriarty, the forty-six-year-old general advertising manager who worked his way up from selling ads right out of high school; and Bella Naropa, the fifty-three-year-old classified manager who also plays in a jazz band. All of these people enjoy their jobs for different reasons and think of the paper as a place of comfort.

During this phase Mike and his administrative staff stay in the office to manage things while his editors take off. Bella goes to New York to be inspired by her favorite jazz clubs. Andrea signs on for a week's writing workshop in Vermont. Dean simply fills up his car and hits the road because he thinks a little cross-country ride might generate some new ideas. Rudy retreats to his cabin in the Adirondacks. They each know this is their last chance and they don't want to let Mike down. They need to maintain the legacy he is trying to carry on and, most important, their own value and income, and that of their colleagues and friends.

Letting Go: Sending Ideas into the Real World

IN PRINCIPLE

For a person to let go of having singular control over how his work is understood and interpreted is a movement from security to insecurity—from comfort to the unknown. Why would anybody want to make that journey? Why not simply hold tight to something that feels perfect within?

"In the instant that Daishinji let go of the paper fish an amazing transformation took place. If Daishinji had not seen it with her own eyes, she would not have believed it." This is why an artist is willing to risk the loss of letting go. Because maybe, just maybe, what she imagines can actually transform into something real. This is the magic of the creative process—a process that completes itself only when the artist is willing to let her creation interact with the real world.

Letting go for Daishinji becomes as important as the act of creating itself. The activity is one in which a mature person, slowly, over time, disappears into her work in a way that there is no separation between work and worker.

Again we have a paradox, that of a worker being so fully present within her work that she disappears, leaving only the creation in her wake. A filmmaker to consider here is Woody Allen, who has made a movie a year for almost forty years. Allen's personality is unmistakable, and his idiosyncrasies have become almost synonymous with his films—his penchant for Freud and New York City and his belief in anti-Semitic conspiracy theories are hallmarks. But in at least three films in recent years, *Match Point* in 2005, *Sweet and Lowdown* in 1999, and *Crimes and Misdemeanors* in 1989, Allen disappeared. I don't mean that he didn't appear on the screen as an actor—he played an important part in *Crimes and Misdemeanors*. What I mean is that in those films his work transcended the personal, and he used his creative talent to produce works of universal impact. The filmmaker merged with his work in a way that his hand could not be seen. The marionette strings of the films' creator had long ago been severed in some private moment of letting go.

Another medium to consider in letting go is dance. Isadora Duncan (1877–1927), known as one of the founders of Modern Dance, said: "If I could tell you what it meant, there would be no point in dancing it." In abandoning herself to the choreography, the master dancer loses her individual personality; there is only movement, flight, and a universal story.

Letting go is the mark of the professional. It is the mark of one willing to love the idea outside more than the small ego within that tends to demand recognition. To witness such movement—this collective activity that overcomes individual differentiation—watch the Radio City Music Hall Rockettes. Each dancer on her own is a well-trained professional, but when you watch the Rockettes perform as a unit it is as though forty bodies have become one. The letting go of personal style is complete and for the sake of a greater good—a communication of precision and power.

A group of talented people who consent to relinquish their individual preferences in favor of creating something bigger is what makes a film, a dance, a play, a concert, and a company possible. The individual talent is not lost but is assigned a purpose—this is what differentiates an audition from a performance. An audition shows us how good an artist is; a performance shows us how true an idea is.

Problems in companies come when management fails to make a person sufficiently comfortable to let go. The result is that the person continues to audition (show off his talent) when he should be performing (expressing the group's mission with universal precision).

IN PRACTICE

Once an individual has come up with an idea that he or she absolutely loves, the next step is to let it go into the world. By guiding people in letting go through first honoring their original creations and ensuring that they have enough autonomous time to tinker with them, the manager can build a team in which ideas become common ground.

As a manager who has cast well, you have a team of talented professionals at your disposal—now what? You have sent these professionals off to use their skills to come up with a solution that no one has ever come up with before. They have now returned from their autonomous quest and it is up to you to lead the way to execution.

You can do this by demonstratively honoring their autonomy. Let each one of them first discuss the creative process without talking yet about the product. Use this time as an opportunity for the team members to gradually let go of the experience they had by acknowledging it in a kind of public ritual. They can be invited to bring photos of the studio/natural environment that provided them inspiration during their autonomous period. This is also a chance for the team members to learn about each other's creative process and become better adept at being sensitive to it every day at work, and not just during these intense autonomous periods. This is an especially important time for you as manager to listen closely. By understanding how your team is inspired you can better equip the work environment to suit the needs of innovation rather than the outmoded remnants of corporate hierarchy.

The first day back after the intense autonomous period is treated as a transition from self to group. It is a transformation akin to a caterpillar about to undergo a metamorphosis into a butterfly—try to open the cocoon a day early and you will defile the entire natural process.

The Exercise

When the group is assembled, each member brings an object associated with his or her creative discovery—not with the product but with the process. An individual who became inspired by spending his mornings working in a pottery studio may bring one of the pots he fired. An individual who drew inspiration from her walks on the beach may bring a seashell or piece of driftwood. Someone who was sparked by a hike up a mountain may bring a rock discovered along the trail; the list goes on depending on the circumstances—the objects can be anything.

What is vital is that after each object is described and honored it is placed in a large wooden box in the center of the group. The group is then given the task of working together with all of these objects to create a single object. The members have to do this work in silence, communicating intuitively through gesture and instinct. When they are finished they take the object and find a prominent place for it within the work space. At this point the group is charged with describing the creation and finding its meaning as a team.

This process mirrors what they later do with their final ideas—collaborate. But first and foremost on this day they collaborate in honoring their collective letting go. Going through this step will make them that much more receptive to respecting each other's results as the process moves forward. Each sees that the other is as individual as he or she is. The goal is for each person's protective shell to give way to the trusted spirit of the group. It is up to the manager to facilitate this process with dignity, trust, and laughter.

THE CASE

On the Monday back after the autonomous week, Mike Holloway arranges for lunch to be brought in and he sets aside the conference room and puts a "do not disturb" sign on the door. After the members of the group speak about how they spent their week, Mike asks Rudy to begin the ritual by placing the object that best symbolizes his process in the center of the table. Rudy hesitates a moment and then pulls out something encased in plastic that looks like it has seen better days. "I spent a lot of the week thinking about what it was like when I first came to the paper," Rudy says. Then he opens the worn plastic and carefully places on the table the first ever issue of the *Maple* that he worked on. It was a 1968 evening edition and Rudy had reported on the local protest of the Vietnam War staged at the high school. The paper was yellowed, the pictures grainy, and all around the table couldn't help but look at it with a bit of reverence. As they study this remnant of their past, they slowly begin to fixate on the paper's slogan, which has long since been abandoned: "*Relevance is our purpose.*"

Andrea Molloy goes next, and out of her bag she pulls a tiny box. When she opens it there is nothing inside. "Every night after the workshops and the readings I'd sit out with some of the others and watch the moon and talk," Andrea says. "I would have brought back the moon, because I think it influenced me the most, but I couldn't, so I brought back a beam in this box. Can you see it?"

Dean starts to laugh hysterically, and Mike gets concerned. The ground rules are that no one can make fun of anyone else's process, no matter what. It could ruin the atmosphere of trust that inspires collaboration. But before Mike lets his worries carry him too far away, Dean pulls out a container of water from his bag: "Moonbeam, meet my ocean," Dean laughs. "I drove all the way to the coast; I hadn't been there since I was a kid. The ocean contains it all—old, new, discarded, cherished—it's all there. And a bit of all of that mixed up inside me and reminded me how what I thought long ago could in fact be the key to creating something brand new now."

Bella goes last and out of her bag she pulls a post-card from a landmark New York jazz club. "These musicians I saw last week were as good as they are, I realized, not because of the way they play, but because of the precision with which they listen. They hear each other and only then respond with a riff of their own. It made me reflect on how important it is to listen to all of you and that I don't a lot of the time."

And there it was—the summation of a week's creative process—the moon, the ocean, jazz, and a 1968 issue of the paper. They look at these things in silence for a long time and see each other in these objects. Finally, Bella picks up her postcard and places it inside Andrea's box. Rudy picks up the box and places it on top of the paper. Dean places his jar of ocean water alongside. Mike watches this movement and eventually speaks: "What would we report in our paper if we heard jazz being played from the moon as a beam that reflected off the ocean?" They all look at each other and laugh. "Well, that's what we have to find out," Mike says. "Good work. I'll see everyone tomorrow." And there it is. The manager has facilitated a transition from personal to public.

Exchange:
The Art of Nurturing a
"Work in Progress"

IN PRINCIPLE

The center spot is the place of letting go—where things open up and ideas become real. To meet at the center spot is not just to meet the creation as it is, but also to meet the creator as she is. The center spot is a place of intimacy, a place where people do more than exchange their ideas; they also exchange their values, aspirations, joys, fears, and loves. They do this not necessarily by talking about it but by listening intimately to another's idea in a way that their whole life is heard in it.

During the period of exchange, Daishinji and the apprentice are knocked overboard out of their boat (zone of safety) and thrown into the real experience of a living idea. Daishinji laughs hard from the joy of having been able to show someone the wonder of her creative world. The apprentice, as the listener of exchange, goes into the ocean with Daishinji and thereby enters Daishinji's world without holding back. She does not step back and judge Daishinji's idea; she swims with it instead. Having had an experience rather than a judgment, the apprentice is open to learning. And at that point of openness the apprentice says: "Please teach me what you know." And Daishinji replies simply, "I just did."

The apprentice wants to learn how imaginary things are made real in the world. But Daishinji, now a master, knows that you cannot teach that to another person; you can only show that person how that experience has manifested in your own life. The exchange is complete because the apprentice wants to know how magic is done and Daishinji says, essentially, "I don't know how it is done, but it is done nonetheless." A person does not have to rationally explain how an idea came to life; he or she simply has to show it, to make the other person feel its presence, not the reason for its presence.

Like the fish that no longer fits in the box, there is nothing to hold on to, only an experience to share.

Few people can attest to this better than Martin Scorsese's longtime film editor, Thelma Schoonmaker. Schoonmaker has worked alongside Scorsese for more than thirty years, and their work together is as alive as ever. She won an Oscar for best editing in 1980 for her work on *Raging Bull* and another in 2004 for *The Aviator*. When asked why she maintains such enthusiasm for working with Scorsese, Schoonmaker said: "You know a master is at the controls. Marty infects people with his enthusiasm and love of film, his high standards, his rejection of anything clichéd, and his beautiful style" (*Home Theater Magazine,* November 2005).

The editor brings pace, refinement, precision, rhythm, tone, and mood to a film. She takes this burst of psychic discipline and emotional force and crafts it into an object of art that is portable. The ambition of an editor is to stop the flow of time and create a series of perfect, eternal, unforgettable moments. One individual gets inside another individual's experience so completely that both can see it from the other's vantage point as well as from a place of objectivity. In the process of exchange the receiver helps the giver communicate something universal as well as personal.

The giver also has a great task. If he trusts the exchange process receiver (which is a prerequisite), then he must open himself to her responses to his work as though he now has a partner. The exchange partner represents the first brush with the world outside the creator's imagination. The giver must hold nothing back. He must be prepared to risk learning that his creation/discovery makes no sense to anyone but him. But this is why the receiver of the exchange process is so crucial. The first receiver is a way station between the internal imagination and the outside world.

Compassion is an important component here. The purpose of exchange is to mirror the other's idea so completely that a person can see it for himself in the light of day. And when he does, he may for the first time see that what in the mine looked like a flawless diamond is now flawed aboveground. If he sees this, you have done your job not because you harped on the flaw, but because you exposed it before the larger world had a chance to see it. In doing so, the receiver of the exchange process is not only of great benefit to the idea's outcome, but, more important in the long run, is of invaluable benefit to the development of the creator.

IN PRACTICE

As a manager you must provide clear instructions on how individuals are to listen in this stage. People are asked not to listen as financial or strategic critics, but instead to simply listen for the rationale of the idea and the cogency with which it is articulated. The listener's job is not to lament or praise; it is to ask the kinds of queries that lead the presenter to clarity of intent. This first controlled brush with the outside world allows a creator to comfortably see her idea in the light of day. After seeing, she will have a chance to self-edit, refine, and enhance the idea before presenting to the full group. A partner does not change the other's ideas, though by undertaking an authentic probing process, perhaps she can help her partner to discover the idea's essence and purpose.

After the successful outcome of the letting-go stage the creative team is now ready to exchange not just the creative process, but creative content as well.

Dialogue should be in the form of open-ended questions rather than critical statements. For example, saying "Can you say more about why copper is the best material for the cylinder?" is an appropriate way of relating, whereas "The plant has never manufactured with copper before" is the kind of response that would cut off a conversation rather than engage the creator to delve further into the reasons behind his idea.

The key is curiosity, not criticism. As a manager you will need to train your team to probe an issue like a child playing "Twenty Questions," learning to relish the fascinating mystery of another person's mind. Most of us are analytically trained to understand an argument for the sake of finding its holes. In the case of the exchange process, the manager must retrain his group to be constructive, not to deconstruct.

The manager needs to model how to be objective without being stern and how to encourage without being conciliatory. In *The Analects*, Confucius wrote: "When the Master was singing in the company of others and liked someone else's song, he always asked to hear it again before joining in"(p. 90). The sentiment here is not to join in with enthusiasm until you fully understand. Sometimes, when we like someone personally, we are apt to want to agree with her prematurely without understanding the intricacies of her idea or viewpoint. The manager has to teach the "middle way" in the exchange process—the way between criticism and advocacy—the way of objective clarification.

THE CASE

Dean and Bella are one exchange pair and Andrea and Rudy are the other. Between Dean and Bella, Dean decides he will go first and proceeds to explain how he has always approached advertising in the past and how that process has evolved over the years. He relays a particular experience that occurred during the course of his road trip that helped bring about his new idea. "I was in my car a lot and found myself, as usual, thinking about buying a new one," Dean said.

"After traveling 800 miles with terrible gas mileage and the constant rattle that mechanics have long ago given up on solving, I finally decided I would buy a new car. So where did I look? Not in our paper, but online. I could comparative shop there, create my own options, and see price differentials instantly. No wonder our auto advertising section, which used to give us such great revenue, has all but dried up. A two-dimensional picture of a single car with a few words of description with a single price is no match for the advertising tools online."

Dean goes on for a while, with Bella probing his intent and direction along the way, and finally Dean comes out with the core of his idea. "Problem with those online sites is that the ones that are supposed to be unbiased are not local, they are national; and the ones that are local are all the biased sites of the individual dealers. What if we offered an objective online auto advertising section that used the objective national tools to compare what our local dealers are offering? This way our readers, in this case, users, would get a real value—a local tool that utilizes the best national ideas available. And with it we create an objective picture of the local auto market. As advertisers we no longer just post; we create value for our readers by providing objective information that can help them, which is a paper's mission, after all."

Dean is clearly excited: "And the best part is we make our money by having the local auto dealers underwrite the whole thing. They are in the same revenue bind we are with all the objective national competition—they need this and will pay for it. And they'll pay more than they ever did for ads, because this tool will truly help them." Dean continues, "Funny thing is, I thought of something like this years ago, but we didn't have the technology to support it then. We do now!" Bella smiles and relates her own story of discovery.

Bella spent the bulk of her week in New York City going to jazz clubs in Manhattan. The whole time she was struck by how much more powerful it was to listen to live jazz rather than the stuff on a CD at home. The interactive experience made all the difference. This got her to thinking about the classified section in the newspaper and its dwindling revenues. She finds it boring compared to national live auction sites on the Internet, where you can see close-up views of a variety of products and bid on them. To Bella, the classified section in print feels like something from the Stone Age in comparison.

"And that's when it hit me," Bella reasons. "People don't just use these sites because they love to shop; they use them because they love to interact. So why couldn't we make it even more personal? Just about everybody owns a video camera and a computer. Why couldn't we accept video classified ads online—local people and local companies showcasing their wares. It would be a form of entertainment for people to view this stuff, like *Funniest Home Videos* or something; people would get creative. And there could be bidding. Everybody would be talking about it. We could charge a couple of bucks per transaction and make a fortune. We wouldn't charge for placement of the ad like we do now. We would charge a service fee to the seller only after the product sold: an incentive-based model; I bet we would clean up. Everybody wants his or her fifteen minutes of fame anyway," Bella says, smiling. "Well, now they'd have it! Live and personal—the classifieds as live jazz."

In another room sit Rudy and Andrea. Rudy is in the middle of explaining how much he enjoyed coming across that first paper where he had a story. Rudy's idea involves preservation that would make the *Maple* not just a paper, but an available library and resource. He calls his idea "Archive Alive," which he explains would be a project to scan all the old newspapers onto a Web server and then bring the content to life by creating links that relate to present-day issues—a kind of internal Google search engine that would be specific to the *Maple* newspaper. "And the links wouldn't be just to other websites or articles, but also to images and relevant real-time media," Rudy explains excitedly. He is thinking of how he hopes to combine his love of the history of the newspaper with his desire to increase the newspaper's accessibility to young readers who think of printed materials as relics.

Andrea listens closely, questioning and asking for clarification where she can. Finally she says, "But Rudy, how do we get new young readers to care about our history if they don't even know us in the present?" Rudy smiles. "Exactly; we have to make our history unbelievably relevant. This is what I mean by 'Archive Alive'—it will be a living history. Rather than using a dusty record room on the fifth floor we could create a media center in the lobby of the paper where the greatest moments in the city's history are right there and available to anybody who walks in the door. We get people invested in this paper again. We show them that they can be a part of something bigger and more meaningful than just some little online community that has been around for three years. I think people want to be a part of something older and more significant than that if we would only give them a way in."

Andrea understands what Rudy is talking about and feels his passion for the newspaper. As news editor her idea isn't that far off. She also wants to generate new support by creating more accessible ways for people to touch the paper. Her idea has two aspects to it. She tells Rudy that the idea came from an exercise she did in one of the fiction-writing workshops. "The instructor showed a series of silent films and when they stopped asked the class to write the dialogue. Lots of great stories came out of it. It got us all into a late-night discussion afterward about the silent film community and what those theaters were like. It got me thinking about our own art-house theater in town and the community that goes to see the films there. We could show newsreels like they used to around World War II—like the 'Archive Alive' idea, Rudy, except I envisioned a kind of 'week in review' on Friday and Saturday nights.

"We wouldn't charge for those of course. But the hope would be that the people at the art-house theater would get the buzz going about the newsreels and that young people would start looking to download them from our website. We're not getting many new young readers, but who is to say we couldn't get lots of new young browsers willing to pay $5.00 for a cool download of the week's events in the place where they live? I think it could work. And I think the readers we already have would love the service, which would come free to them if they renew for a year instead of just twenty-six weeks at a time." Andrea is thrilled. Rudy sees a whole new side of her and he likes it. He likes the idea of his archive on those newsreels too.

At the end of the exchange the group of four come back to the main conference room to meet with Mike. The room is bubbling over with energy, and each takes a turn describing how helpful the process was in clarifying the various ideas. They each feel that collaboration is the natural next step. Mike is appreciative, though he can't help but continue to worry about the execution phase.

Collaboration: Marrying Creativity with Practical Application

IN PRINCIPLE

One might argue that in the theater nothing ever becomes real—that in fact the playwright creates an imagined world on paper that the director translates into a three-dimensional imagined world on the stage. In other words, in the theater, a paper fish never swims in a real ocean.

But the theater, when executed in the spirit of selfless collaboration, does indeed become real. The transformation of imagination to reality needs the public space to occur—the paper fish of the theater can become real only in the heart of the audience. The audience is the fish that swims out of the theater. Good theater is a mirror; collaboration of this order brings everyone's talents and efforts to one clear, sharp point—an arrow destined to hit its target.

Great actors never seem to be acting; rather, they appear to be simply living their lives on the stage without self-consciousness or pretense. An actor is not a messenger or mouthpiece for the playwright. A good actor makes the play real. This is another side of the paper fish. The actor is the paper fish arguing with Daishinji to be let go to swim in the real ocean—the center spot—the public sphere. With the actor's skill and heart the transformation from paper to flesh is attempted. If the creation is true enough, the ocean (public sphere) will accept it as real and the fish will swim. The audience helps enact the actor's reality and a kind of reciprocal dance takes place, a communication that is purely experiential, like the apprentice being so overwhelmed by the real fish's size and power that she is knocked overboard into the sea to swim with it. In this act, all doubt that the imagination cannot make things real is extinguished.

You can also understand collaboration through the very thing you are using at this minute to comprehend what is on this page. To bend your legs just the right way to sit and read, to position your arms not only to hold the book but also to keep it at the optimum distance from your eyes so you can read the words is a magnificent dance of collaborative effort. This is to say nothing of the higher processing it takes to read the words and give them instant meaning based on the content and context of your past experience, knowledge, and prejudices. Every action you take is a work of collaborative mastery so practiced that most of the time you don't even notice the precision with which your brain serves you.

It may seem that an independent actor controls the body and mind, but really it is the work of tens of billions of interdependent neurons communicating by the nanosecond from axon to dendrite across the open space of the synaptic gap. We notice certain misfires from time to time; we forget a word or the direction we came from, or as a consequence of a long period of sitting our leg may "fall asleep" and temporarily forget how to best serve us. But for the most part, these are blips on the screen. But if we have ever had a heart attack, experienced any degree of aphasia, paralysis, or any another disease or trauma that affects our body and brain's interconnected synchronicity we know that independent will alone does not control us; a collaborative agreement does.

IN PRACTICE

After a thorough exchange of ideas has taken place and all participants have had a chance to be heard and been given adequate time to further hone their ideas, collaboration in a group setting can happen. The managers themselves are now charged with asking the probing questions—not just about the concept but also about the practicality of its execution. In so doing, the tactic is not to put one person on the "hot seat"; on the contrary, the manager expects that the rest of the team will come to the aid of the idea on the table for the moment. The focus here is on discovering the merits of an idea and working diligently to see if this thing on paper can possibly live in reality. In this exercise, management does not rate only the merit of the ideas that individuals come up with on their own; it also rates, with as much weight, the ingenuity and vigor with which team members bring their colleagues' ideas to life.

Collaboration is the ultimate goal of the exercise, not a hoped-for side effect. The most recently available research studies on innovation point out that competition by itself is not as effective as collaboration. Not everyone will have a great "first thought" all the time—inspiration doesn't play favorites. A manager who can assemble a team whose members truly know how to help each other and recognize an inspired idea and build upon it is more valuable than one individual competitive "star."

In the collaborative phase the manager behaves as an external stimulus providing the brain's collaborative potential with an objective function. The manager is likewise the theater director shaping the talent of her team to serve the goal of making the play real in the life of the audience. The manager is the fire that tempers the steel of a work in progress—an objective force for creativity to react against and gain strength and perspective from.

Like Daishinji herself, the manager must be content to have "nothing" to show for his labor, to be a person not in search of the award but rather one in search of the idea's lifeblood. He must be as motivated by the creative process as his team—even more so if the collaborative phase is to be an enriching experience for everyone. If the manager falters in this stage and gets caught up with the result too early, all is lost. It would be like a director spending a rehearsal thinking of the applause of the audience rather than the portrayal of truth in the moment.

The Daishinji manager knows that leadership is the ability to disappear so completely into the purpose of the activity that the team being led sees no personal subjective leader, only the direction inside them being urged to find a place in the world. The manager at her best is a gateway for the team—the person through which the imagined is facilitated into the real.

The process itself involves more than the standard brainstorming session, in which a facilitator stands in front of the room with colored markers and poster paper furiously scribbling ideas and then pasting the pages all over the room for the team to peruse and ultimately do nothing about. These kinds of prototypical sessions, if you get lucky, may jump-start the kernel of an idea but will never serve to develop a sustainable living reality. The collaborative phase of the Paper Fish Process involves the manager having the individuals on the team draw numbers from a hat on the given day of presentation. Each individual presentation is allotted a total of two hours. One hour for the presenter and one hour for the group to question, probe, and try to make the idea work as best they can.

No criticism is allowed. The entire purpose of the exercise is to see if the idea can work realistically. If after open-ended questioning, the team still cannot see a way to build on the idea to make it real then silence is appropriate. Silence spurs thought whereas criticism kills creativity. If the group is silent for more than ten minutes then the manager can call for a silent walking break outside (rain or shine); usually something outside the office environment will spark a new thought. There is a forty-five-minute break after the first hour of presentation and scheduled ten-minute breaks after each one-hour session of questioning, probing, and idea building. Each workday allows for no more than two presentations.

The Daishinji manager is a strict timekeeper and an enforcer of the ground rules, which are as follows:

1. Participate in every session.

2. Question; do not criticize.

3. Speak one at a time.

4. Do not lie; silence is better.

After a few sessions, if the Daishinji manager is modeling her job well, the rules will be internalized and the team will become self-regulating.

As for the presenter, the rules are:

1. Do not use standard PowerPoint.

2. Show the idea; do not just describe it (think of the apprentice being thrown overboard when Daishinji showed her "idea").

3. Limit the presentation budget to an agreed-upon amount per presenter.

Within the boundaries of these rules there is room for infinite creativity.

Have you ever watched a Hollywood blockbuster that was absolutely terrible despite the millions of dollars spent on production value? If a compelling story is not present and a reason for its being not evident then all production value ends up as smoke and mirrors, wasted money for the producers, an embarrassment for the actors, and a shame for the audience. On the other hand, have you ever gone to a community theater and paid about ten bucks for your ticket and been brought to tears by the heartfelt acting of unknown actors dressed in black playing with the technical support of no more than a few spotlights? You can't buy creativity, only a camouflage to try to mask its lack.

Let's take an even closer-to-home example for business life. Have you ever hired a top advertising agency to show you a new campaign only to come home and talk to your eleven-year-old daughter about the idea and go to sleep wishing you had checked with her first before plunking down that exorbitant agency fee? In other words, true creaviy is the demonstration of heart and originality, not flash. The rules exist to keep focused on that.

If the team members seem anything less than sharp throughout this process, give them a break. Send them to the gym for a workout or to a park to watch the changing light on the trees. Ask them to come back tomorrow refreshed. If they can't be present in mind and body they do not deserve to be on the team—it is disrespectful to the others who are working so hard. There is a difference between fatigue and indifference and the Daishinji manager is well aware of how each manifests. Fatigue has a remedy; indifference is inexcusable.

The Daishinji manager, in the collaboration phase of the process, is chief facilitator and coach, not judge or critic. Her job is to set up an atmosphere for an honest, open, and engaged collaboration. She keeps to a strict time schedule, keeps the group well fed and rested, watches for fatigue and/or indifference, enforces the rules when necessary, and knows when to encourage further questioning/probing and, likewise, when to keep quiet.

All sessions should be videotaped and then transcribed as quickly as possible. After the collaborative phase of the process is complete, the team members should feel more deeply connected to their own ideas, to each other, and to the organization as a whole. They should know themselves, how they work, and how others work. A Daishinji manager is looking to build a team the way John Wooden and Phil Jackson did—for the long haul. Individuals who become a team do better work together; they develop a kind of short-hand with each other. Their collective ideas get better over time as they learn to effectively help each other.

This is the impact a thoughtful manager can make—to build a team that seems like it can win all by itself without a coach. The best teams are always like this—it seems like the coach is being paid simply to watch. And he is . . . but he is watching so he can better observe how to subtly teach the players how to help themselves and each other. A great coach strives to make his presence unnecessary on the field; it is the same with a Daishinji manager during the collaborative part of the process.

THE CASE

Mike Holloway listens intently as Rudy describes his "Archive Alive," Bella her interactive classifieds, Dean his online transparently priced local car lot, and Andrea her newsreels. And after these brief explanations, they each show a sample of what they mean with the help of undergraduate students who were each the recipient of a $300 grant from the paper made to the local university's burgeoning multimedia department. Each idea seems to build on the other. Dean suggests that after hearing Bella's idea again he thinks the online auto ads could actually be more like an online auction with competitive bidding that would make for a more interactive feel.

All the participants express great excitement that their autonomous thinking has produced so much potential for interactive synergy. The group comes back together after the second day and Rudy has a gigantic smile on his face. "What is it?" asks Andrea. "I was just thinking," says Rudy. "I remembered some of the things Dave McKay, my first publisher at this paper, used to talk about when he ran the paper in the late 1960s and 1970s."

Rudy addresses Mike Holloway directly now. "See, Mike, Dave's vision was that we create a paper that people wanted to read aloud at the barbershop, on the street corner, wherever—he always talked about it as a public community thing, not as a private experience. It's funny, I thought I knew what he meant then, but I know what he meant even more now. These interactive experiences we're all talking about will become this communal experience that Dave used to preach about. Technology does not have to alienate us. We just have to know how to use it for a communal purpose. Could it be that we are actually going to execute our purpose better than ever because we will begin to use the tools that we thought of as the domain of our competitors?"

Mike Holloway pauses a while then says, "Dave never told me that when I took over." "It was a long time ago," Rudy says. "It was the kind of thing that came out in a flash of after-hour inspiration that got forgotten in the morning." The team is silent as Mike proceeds to speak about how he has been struggling with the best way to carry on the legacy of the paper while keeping it profitable. The team has not seen Mike this open in months. Fear is giving way to purpose, and the imagined is becoming more real.

Innovation:
From Paper to Flesh

IN PRINCIPLE

Had Daishinji brought the paper fish to the ocean before it ever spoke or demanded life, she would have risked crushing her idea before it was strong enough to live on its own. At the other extreme, had Daishinji refused ever to take the paper fish out to the ocean, nothing would have been risked, but neither would anything have been gained. Innovation is that transformative act where the imagined becomes real. As hard as it is, Daishinji must risk failure and be accountable. She must go into the real world and find out if her idea can live. So it is for the manager. He must take the positive collaboration of his team and see whether it actually has legs to stand on.

Creativity is the realm of the team; the manager is now charged with taking the sum of that creative exploration and effort and turning it into innovation for the company. Creativity is a process and innovation is a result.

The transformation from successful creative process to marketable innovative result is the stage in which the Daishinji manager moves from being a facilitator to being a decision maker. A few connected analogies will help us arrive at a thorough understanding of the work ahead. Let us return to the life of a film editor of the caliber of Martin Scorsese's longtime colleague Thelma Schoonmaker. Schoonmaker does not often appear on the set of a movie. She prefers to focus on the objective reality of viewing the footage alone and in private. When the filming has been done and the actors and crew go home, the editor is left with an enormous job. She must take all the footage, the score, the additional music, and the b-roll (additional shots of scenery not part of the main narrative), and from these hours of labor create a coherent film that is a work of art, is marketable to the general public, and, in Schoonmaker's case, makes a noticeable innovative impact on the world of film. All of this occurs after the creative team on the set has worked selflessly and passionately. The editor must convert a process into a realized, portable product that can be distributed worldwide.

The editor cannot begin with the question, "How do I make this film a profitable one?" If she does, she will find no truth in it. Questions like that must come later down the line when the marketing component gets involved. The editor's concern is how to make all of the footage converge into one tightly realized idea. The editor's craft is to trim the excess and find the essential—to trace the connecting symbols, themes, dialogue, and movement of the work and allow it to speak for itself as a unified whole. Often an actor or director's favorite scenes are cut, not because they are not excellent scenes, but because they do not fit the overarching purpose of the film when all is said and done. The editing process can be painful to the director and cast as the editor extracts the marrow and pares the fat, but it can also be an ecstatic process as a director or an actor discovers a truth previously unknown to him.

When the editor has finished her work a product exists, where before there was only a process. An editor is like the sculptor who takes a large piece of marble with all of its potential and carves it into a recognizable form that people can see and grasp at once. The audience will have to understand the heart of the creative team's efforts through a single finite product, and this reality can be difficult to accept for a creative person who has invested herself for so many hours and days in the imagined and thereby infinite world of the creative process. The editor mediates the transition from process to product, and this responsibility is an awesome one.

Innovation is a powerful kind of alchemy because it gives birth while it simultaneously kills. The paradox of the groundbreaking innovation of the gas-powered automobile is worth considering. Nikolaus August Otto invented the gas motor engine in 1876. Gottlieb Daimler invented a gas engine that allowed for a revolution in car design in 1885. That same year, Karl Benz built the first-ever practical automobile to be powered by an internal combustion engine. In 1891, John Lambert invented the first gas-powered automobile in America. By 1908, Henry Ford had popularized the gas-powered automobile through his masterful assembly line production technology. In 1908, a Ford Model T cost $950 and took 923 minutes to make; by 1927, the car cost $280 and took only 23 minutes to make. The result was that cars quickly became the mode of transport for the masses in America.

Among the ripples from that stone being cast into

the ocean of the world were the breakdown of the normal workday and the creation of a three-shift twenty-four-hour-a-day production facility that never shut down. This breakdown created a workforce that struggled to find time with family. The nature of assembly line work itself produced workers from whom no creativity was asked. Monotonous mind-numbing work was the consequence for millions of workers who were and are the product of Ford's innovative process. Additionally, Ford's innovation gave rise to the creation of suburbia, malls, a highway system that destroys landscapes and pristine views at will, and a lifestyle categorized by motion without appropriate consideration of the reason for the effort expended in motion.

The irony is that Ford (1863–1947) lived to regret what his innovation had unleashed. He spent considerable effort and money in the latter part of his life on restoring an idyllic agrarian town called Greenfield Village, a town that resembled the one of his youth—a life before his innovation took hold.

The lesson is that while the creative process is extraordinarily fun, playful, malleable, and flowing, the metamorphosis into innovation is as dangerous as it is thrilling. Innovation is what turns the wheel of the future. Its ripples cannot be seen by the original innovator, but they will surely be felt by her descendants.

Innovation is like Pandora's Box. The overly cautious are useless but the reckless are dangerous; the Daishinji manager walks the middle way.

IN PRACTICE

After the creative team has had a chance to collaborate on the best ideas it is up to the manager to determine how these best ideas can be positioned as innovations within the company's internal processes or external market space. The manager has now used her greatest resources in the company—the minds on the team. She is now charged with converting that intellectual capital into working capital for the company. The manager must now use her gifts, her business acumen, to transfer ideas into innovations that will enhance the company's bottom-line value for all stakeholders.

Management has a clear process by which to put its greatest assets to work for, and the team has an outlet to dream big and be heard by management—everyone has a place at the table. Creativity and the bottom line no longer need live in opposition. They can meet on the shared road of innovation and see how much they need each other to produce real-world results. Too often in the workplace there is an "us" and "them" mentality. This can happen between marketing and sales, management and frontline staff, or the creative staff and management. The Daishinji manager cuts through that traditional paradigm by honoring the mystery and wonder of the creative process.

We will continue with the analogy of a film editor of a commercial film. When the editor's job is done, the work has to travel a great distance from the original creative process and be scrutinized for its marketable properties, financial projections, and the business development that will be needed for distribution, advertising, promotion, product development (features on the DVD, soundtrack, etc.), product placements, and co-promotions. This is the time and place in which the creative process gives way entirely to the business plan for a new product. At the stage of innovation the manager is charged with being not only the editor, but also the lead marketer, distributor, alliance manager, business developer, and product manager. All of these tasks must be taken up in sequence. Rushing to them is the equivalent of taking a chocolate cake out of the oven before it has had a chance to bake and eating it—you end up with a mouth full of flour, sugar, eggs, milk, salt, baking soda, vanilla, and cocoa, but what you taste is nothing that resembles the taste of a chocolate cake.

After the collaborative creative process is over and all the video footage of the sessions has been transcribed, it is time for the manager to go to work. The manager's first job is to act as film editor—to look through everything in search of what fits together. Are these eight short films or one long feature? Who are the protagonists and why? Which scenes will have to be cut because they do not suit the central innovative goal?

The editing job at this stage of transformation from creativity to innovation is more like that of a traditional documentary film editor than a feature film editor. A feature film editor has a script that he follows. A documentary film editor has hours of footage on a given topic that he has to realize in the form of a coherent theme. The Daishinji manager, armed with her tapes and transcripts, is going off to perform the alchemy of turning the documentation of the creative process into a viable business innovation. This is no small feat. Daishinji managers need to be not only expert facilitators but also analytical, intuitive, and decisive in their own right.

For too long, managers have been relegated to the role of bureaucrat driving voicemail and e-mail and meetings with the posture of generic corporate representation. Daishinji managers are not interested in that role—they instead step out from the bureaucratic pose and use their mind and guts to think through complex problems. They fail or succeed based on the content of their analysis and are ready to accept the consequences openly.

The Daishinji manager converts process to product. During that time he does not respond to e-mails or phone calls; he is engaged in the most important job he was hired to do—to transform human talent into fuel for the company's growth and improvement. The manager should take as much time as he needs to execute this process, but he must act.

The manager then works with people from business development, financial, marketing, public relations, distribution, legal, regulatory, governmental affairs, and any other department deemed necessary by the given industry to help understand and execute the team's innovation.

With the help of these specialists the manager develops a plan for bringing the innovation to market. When the plan is ready it is then presented back to the original team so the team can execute it.

Moving from thinking about something to executing it requires a careful transition that the manager must be sensitive about. When a person watches his paper fish swim it is a simultaneous moment of rapture and of loss. The reality of a thing will never be as perfect as our imagined vision of it. When the imagined thing becomes real, we the creator are not needed as we once were. The Daishinji in all of us must turn around from that center spot and go home in an empty boat. The thing we imagined has been transformed, and if we have paid attention, so have we.

THE CASE

Mike Holloway gets the technical help he needs from corporate to build one of the most creative websites in the newspaper business. Andrea has worked diligently with the city's public access cable station to help her produce newsreel weeks in review, and the local buzz does spread until tens of thousands of users are driven to the *Maple* website to download content for which they are willing to pay. Bella hires the university's top graduate in Web development and gets her to design the most creative online classified section anyone has ever seen. It is a cross between a chat room and a home shopping network; it is driven by the consumers and they love it for that reason and are thus willing to pay a service fee when they sell their products. Dean not only does his online auto auction, but he also converts the idea into an objective real estate site at which the paper itself sells MLS numbers and acts as a kind of online realtor for those users not inclined to pay 6 percent of their home price to a traditional realtor. The online newspaper realty service utilizes MLS tools and county property records to conduct comparative price searches for a reasonable fee that provides tremendous revenue growth to the paper. Rudy's "Archive Alive" is up and running, and multimedia interns are working on bringing those past issues to life the way the current issue lives. Each month a different volume from the archive is featured in the open storefront where the dusty lobby of the paper used to be.

Mike has found a way to turn a profit at the paper by charging a "subscription fee" for the downloadable version of various parts of the *Maple* that are relevant to people's lives. Mike sends his top reporters and editors to school one evening a week to train in multimedia and content management, and the local university has established a large internship program at the *Maple* where multimedia artists learn how to interact with substantive content that they can enhance through their skill. The multinational corporate parent is pleased, but even more important, Mike's people are excited. They have saved their own jobs and the life of a great newspaper. They also feel that they have found a way to leap into the future in an innovative manner while preserving what was most worthwhile in the legacy of the *Maple*. And this is what is most exciting about the Paper Fish Process. The essential love—the living flesh of the black and white newsprint that smudges your hands and makes a real sound when you turn its pages—has come back to life with the help of nonprint complementary improvements. Through this process, what is most valued is not discarded or exchanged; it is revitalized and reborn.

A Final Thought

The paper fish swims because it changes into what the ocean requires. Without adaptation, an idea might be pure, but it will be worthless—just a paper fish in a red box. But with adaptation what is beautiful can also become functional. The offspring of the idea and the pragmatic is life as we know it. If we had only the idea we would have no physical reality to exist within; with only the pragmatic we would have no dream. It is this desire to take an idea and shape it into a real thing that creates the world as we know it. And as we create the world, we simultaneously create ourselves.

Ten Situations in Which the Paper Fish Process Can Be Applied

1. You are a product manager of a pharmaceutical company getting ready to launch a new product; meanwhile, your competitor has launched a product just like yours but without the negative side effect that your product has.

2. You are the CEO of a privately held company that has been successful for many years. You are about to go public, and your team is anxious about what this means.

3. You are the manager of a design team at an American automaker that has made its mark by designing

SUVs that look like tanks and get similar gas mileage to that of a tank. Gas prices have doubled, however, and oil is scarce.

4. You are a VP of a major North American airline in charge of managing one of the main hubs. Your competitors that are making money while you lose it are operating successfully without hubs. They have a different business model entirely and yours feels outdated and burdensome.

5. You are the sergeant of a police force facing increased violence among youths ages 12–15 between the hours of 3 P.M. and 6 P.M. on the corner of 5th and Vine.

6. You own a chain of grocery stores and you strive to provide freshness and quality at a reasonable price. You have been operating at a profit for twelve years, but this has begun to change in the locales where a Super Wal-Mart is operating.

7. You are a commercial developer and the 1,600-acre development you have under way turns out to be based on a mistaken survey. Five million dollars into the investment in the project you learn that the industrial park you built actually sits on an easement owned by the city.

8. You run a call center for a global apparel manufacturer. Your customer service ratings have always been high, but since you began outsourcing, your numbers are up but your ratings are down.

9. You are the North American leader of a major insurance company, and your research team clarifies your assumption about how underinsured the majority of American workers are in the area of long-term care and disability. As much as you have tried to communicate the crisis given the aging population, your people have been unsuccessful in turning these vital statistics into results for the company.

10. You are the president of a national mortgage company, and as rates adjust upward, the people who got ARMs five years ago are having to refinance. You are being faced with more foreclosures than ever.

Getting Started with Your Own Team

For some managers and teams this process is going to come naturally, and you will see the way to translate it from this book into your own practice. For others, the challenges will be especially complex and further assistance will be needed.

The Paper Fish Process is an ongoing learning experience for those of us who have committed to going through it. Please feel free to share your learning/questions with me at www.paperfishprocess.com as well as to utilize the tools that are posted online.

Recommended Reading

Adaptors and innovators: styles of creativity and problem-solving. (ed. Kirton, Michael J.). London; New York: Routledge, 1989.

Addis, William. *Creativity and innovation: the structural engineer's contribution to design.* Oxford; Boston: Architectural Press, 2001.

The advertising business: operations, creativity, media planning, integrated communications. (ed. Jones, John Philip). Thousand Oaks, Calif.: Sage Publications, 1999.

Amabile, Teresa. *The social psychology of creativity.* New York: Springer-Verlag, 1983.

Bedford, Mitchell. *Existentialism and creativity.* New York: Philosophical Library, 1972.

Brooke-Rose, Christine. *Stories, theories, and things.* Cambridge, England; New York: Cambridge University Press, 1991.

Campbell, Don G. *The Mozart effect for children: awakening your child's mind, health, and creativity with music.* New York: William Morrow, 2000.

Carney, Thomas P. *False profits: the decline of industrial creativity.* Notre Dame, Ind.: University of Notre Dame Press, 1981.

Chang, Chung-yuan. *Creativity and Taosim: a study of Chinese philosophy, art & poetry.* New York: Harper & Row, 1963, 1970.

Recommended Reading

A Chinese literary mind: culture, creativity and rhetoric in Wenxin Diaolong. (ed. Cai, Zong-qi). Stanford: Stanford University Press, 2001.

Cohen, Gene D. *The creative age: awakening human potential in the second half of life.* New York: Avon Books, 2000.

Coleman, Earle Jerome. *Creativity and spirituality: bonds between art and religion.* Albany: State University of New York Press, 1998.

Community of creativity: a century of MacDowell Colony artists. (org. Spahr, P. Andrew; frwd. Banks, William Nathaniel; cont. Storr, Robert; Wolf, Tom). Manchester, N.H.: The Currier Gallery of Art, 1996.

Creativity & madness: psychological studies of art and artists. (ed. Panter, Barry, et al.). Burbank, Calif.: Aimed Press, 1995.

Creativity and moral vision in psychology: narratives on identity and commitment in a postmodern age. (ed. Tsoi Hoshmand, Lisa). Thousand Oaks, Calif.: Sage Publications, 1998.

Creativity assessment: readings and resources. (eds. Puccio, Gerard J.; Murdock, Mary C.). Buffalo, N.Y.: Creative Education Foundation Press, 1999.

Creativity in performance. (ed. Sawyer, R. Keith). Greenwich, Conn.: Ablex, 1997.

Creativity in the arts and science. (eds. Shea, William R.; Spadafora, Antonio). Canton, Mass.: Science History Publications U.S.A., 1990.

Csikszentmihalyi, Mihaly. *Creativity: flow and the psychology of discovery and invention.* New York: HarperCollins Publishers, 1996.

Dacey, John S. *Understanding creativity: the interplay of biological, psychological, and social factors.* (ed. Lennon, Kathleen). San Francisco: Jossey-Bass, 1998.

Dasgupta, Subrata. *Creativity in invention and design: computational and cognitive explorations of technological originality.* Cambridge, England; New York: Cambridge University Press, 1994.

Dasgupta, Subrata. *Technology and creativity.* New York: Oxford University Press, 1996.

Davis, Gary A. *Study guide and creativity exercises to accompany Creativity is forever, third edition.* (eds. Glover, John A.; Ronning, Royce R.; Reynolds, Cecil R.). Dubuque, Iowa: Kendall/Hunt Pub., 1994.

Recommended Reading

De Bono, Edward. *Lateral thinking: creativity step by step.* New York: Perennial Library, 1970, 1973.

De Bono, Edward. *Serious creativity: using the power of lateral thinking to create new ideas.* New York: HarperBusiness, 1992.

Deri, Susan K. *Symbolization and creativity.* New York: International Universities Press, 1984.

Dervin, Daniel. *Creativity and culture: a psychoanalytic study of the creative process in the arts, sciences, and culture.* Rutherford: Fairleigh Dickinson University Press; London: Associated University Presses, 1990.

Dimensions of creativity. (ed. Margaret A. Boden). Cambridge, Mass.: MIT Press, 1994.

Dundon, Elaine. *The seeds of innovation: cultivating the synergy that fosters new ideas.* New York: AMACOM, 2002.

Edwards, Betty. *Drawing on the right side of the brain: a course in enhancing creativity and artistic confidence.* Los Angeles; New York: J.P. Tarcher; dist. St. Martin's Press, 1979.

Eiffert, Stephen D. *Cross-train your brain: a mental fitness program for maximizing creativity and achieving success.* New York: AMACOM, 1999.

Epstein, Robert. *Creativity games for trainers: a handbook of group activities for jumpstarting workplace creativity.* New York: Training McGraw-Hill, 1996.

Eysenck, H. J. (Hans Jurgen). *Genius: the natural history of creativity.* Cambridge, England; New York: Cambridge University Press, 1995.

Freeman, Mark Philip. *Finding the muse: a sociopsychological inquiry into the conditions of artistic creativity.* Cambridge, England; New York: Cambridge University Press, 1993.

Gardner, Howard. *Art, mind, and brain: a cognitive approach to creativity.* New York: Basic Books, 1982.

Gardner, Howard. *Creating minds: an anatomy of creativity seen through the lives of Freud, Einstein, Picasso, Stravinsky, Eliot, Graham, and Gandhi.* New York: BasicBooks, 1993.

Generating creativity and innovation in large bureaucracies. (ed. Kuhn, Robert Lawrence). Westport, Conn.: Quorum Books, 1993.

Recommended Reading

Genius and eminence: the social psychology of creativity and exceptional achievement. (ed. Albert, Robert S.). Oxford; New York: Pergamon Press, 1983.

Genius and the mind: studies of creativity and temperament. (ed. Steptoe, Andrew). Oxford; New York: Oxford University Press, 1998.

Handbook of creativity. (ed. Sternberg, Robert J.). Cambridge, England; New York: Cambridge University Press, 1999.

Hare, A. Paul (Alexander Paul). *Creativity in small groups.* Beverly Hills, Calif.: Sage Publications, 1981.

Holbrook, David. *Creativity and popular culture.* Rutherford: Fairleigh Dickinson University Press; London: Associated University Press, 1994.

Innovation and creativity at work: psychological and organizational strategies. (eds. West, Michael A.; Farr, James L.). Chichester, England; New York: Wiley, 1990.

Intelligence: reconceptualization and measurement. (ed. Rowe, Helga A. H.). Hillsdale, N.J.: Erlbaum Associates, 1991.

Inventive minds: creativity in technology. (eds. Weber, Robert J.; Perkins, David N.). New York: Oxford University Press, 1992.

Jungerman, John A. *World in process: creativity and interconnection in the new physics.* (frwd. Cobb, John B.). Albany: State University of New York Press, 2000.

Kay, Ronald. *Managing creativity in science and hi-tech.* Berlin; New York: Springer-Verlag, 1990.

Klinger, Eric. *Daydreaming: your hidden resource for self-knowledge and creativity.* Los Angeles: J.P. Tarcher, 1990.

Kolodny, Susan. *The captive muse: on creativity and its inhibition.* Madison, Conn.: Psychosocial Press, 2000.

Kuntsler, Barton Lee. *The hothouse effect: intensify creativity in your organization using secrets from history's most innovative communities.* New York: AMA-COM, 2004.

Lampikoski, Kari. *Igniting innovation: inspiring organizations by managing creativity.* (ed. Emden, Jack B.). Chichester, England; New York: Wiley, 1996.

Recommended Reading

Lee, V. J. (Victor J.). *Creativity.* (cont. Williams, Phillip). Bletchley, England: The Open University Press, 1972.

Leonard-Barton, Dorothy. *When sparks fly: igniting creativity in groups.* (ed. Swap, Walter C.). Boston, Mass.: Harvard Business School Press, 1999.

Li, Rex. *A theory of conceptual intelligence: thinking, learning, creativity, and giftedness.* Westport, Conn.: Praeger, 1996.

Lieberman, Josefa Nina. *Playfulness: its relationship to imagination and creativity.* New York: Academic Press, 1977.

Meyer, Pamela. *Quantum creativity: nine principles to transform the way you work.* Lincolnwood, Ill.: Contemporary Books, 2000.

Miller, Arthur I. *Insights of genius: imagery and creativity in science and art.* New York: Copernicus, 1996.

Morgan, Ronald R. *Rethinking creativity.* (eds. Ponticell, Judith A.; Gordon, Edward E.). Bloomington, Ind.: Phi Delta Kappa Educational Foundation, 2000.

The Nature of creativity: contemporary psychological perspectives. (ed. Sternberg., Robert J.). Cambridge, England; New York: Cambridge University Press, 1988.

Nettle, Daniel. *Strong imagination: madness, creativity and human nature.* Oxford: Oxford University Press, 2001.

O'Connor, Joseph. *The art of systems thinking: essential skills for creativity and problem solving.* (ed. McDermott, Ian). London: Thorsons, 1997.

The origins of creativity. (eds. Pfenninger, Karl H.; Shubik, Valerie R.; cont. Adolphe, Bruce). Oxford; New York: Oxford University Press, 2001.

Perry, Susan K. *Writing in flow: keys to enhanced creativity.* Cincinnati, Ohio: Writer's Digest Books, 1999.

Piirto, Jane. *Understanding those who create.* Dayton, Ohio: Ohio Psychology Press, 1992.

The power of play: new visions of creativity. (ed. Lawson, Carol S.). West Chester, Pa.: Chrysalis Books, 1996.

Recommended Reading

Prince, George M. *The practice of creativity; a manual for dynamic group problem solving.* New York: Harper & Row, 1970.

Rabe, Cynthia Barton. *The innovation killer: how what we know limits what we can imagine—and what smart companies are doing about it.* New York: AMACOM, 2006.

Ray, Michael L. *Creativity in business.* (ed. Myers, Rochelle). New York: Doubleday, 1989.

Ricchiuto, Jack. *Collaborative creativity: unleashing the power of shared thinking.* Akron, Ohio: Oakhill Press, 1997.

Rickards, Tudor. *Creativity and the management of change.* Oxford, England; Malden, Mass.: Blackwell Publishers, 1999.

Sanders, Donald A. *Teaching creativity through metaphor: an integrated brain approach.* (ed. Sanders, Judith A.). New York: Longman, 1984.

Steptoe, John. *Creativity.* (ill. Lewis, Earl B.). New York: Clarion Books, 1997.

Theories of creativity. (eds. Runco, Mark A.; Albert, Robert S.). Newbury Park: Sage Publications, 1990.

Thinking and problem solving. (ed. Sternberg., Robert J.). San Diego: Academic Press, 1994.

Turner, Scott R. *The creative process: a computer model of storytelling and creativity.* Hillsdale, N.J.: L. Erlbaum, 1994.

Weiner, Robert. *Creativity & beyond: cultures, values, and change.* Albany: State University of New York Press, 2000.

Weintraub, Sandra. *The hidden intelligence: innovation through intuition.* Boston: Butterworth-Heinemann, 1998.

Weisberg, Robert W. *Creativity: genius and other myths.* New York: W.H. Freeman, 1986.

Index

accountability, 78, 115–116
"action-potentials," ideas as, 64
actions, perceptive reality altered by, 63–64
actors, 104
adaptation, 127
added value, from each person's creativity, 59
administrative efficiency, 66
alchemy, innovation as, 118
Allen, Woody, 82–83
Amabile, Teresa, on stifling creativity, 74
Analects, The (Confucius), 96
arts, 57
atmosphere, creating, 65–66
attitude for innovation, 56
automobiles, 118–119
autonomy, 71–79
   in creative process, 72–73, 75
   creativity and need for, 74
   and early tentativeness of ideas, 73–74
   honoring, 85
   manager's role in, 75–78
   in *Maple* newspaper case, 78–79
   paradox of, 72
Aviator, The (film), 93

Benz, Karl, 118
best practices for creative process, 57
brainstorming, collaboration vs., 108
business plan, 121

cars, manufacturing, 118–119
center spot, 91
"close monitoring," 74
coach, manager as, 111, 112
collaboration, 86–87, 103–114
   brainstorming vs., 108
   criticism in process of, 108
   exercise for, 108–110
   ground rules for, 109–110
   in group setting, 106
   in human body, 104–105
   manager's role in, 106–112
   in *Maple* newspaper case, 112–114
   transformation of imagination to reality in, 103–104
compassion, in exchange stage, 94
competent functionality, 65
Confucius, 96
consultancy, team as, 59–60
control
   of creativity, 76
   of ideas, 62
   letting go of, *see* letting go
   of time in autonomy stage, 74–76
co-workers, creative, 74
creative consultancy, team as, 59–60
creative power, control of, 71–72
creative process, 57
   autonomy in, 72–73, 75
   best practices for, 57
   in groups, 73, 74

Index

creative process (*continued*)
honoring, 121
listening to ideas in, 62
manager as protector of, 75
metamorphosed into innovation, 119–120
need for space and time in, 73–74
creativity
in all employees, 59
areas of, 57
atmosphere for, 65–66
control of, 76
environment fostering, 56
and need for autonomy, 74
stifling, 74
"Creativity on the Clock" (*Monitor on Psychology*), 74
creators
creations as creators of, 73
as mediators of inspiration, 62
time alone needed by, 71–72
Crimes and Misdemeanors (film), 82
criticism, 95–96, 108
culture of innovation, *see* innovation culture
curiosity, 64, 95–96

daily practice of creativity, 67
Daimler, Gottlieb, 118
Daishinji Journal, 67
"Daishinji management," *see* Paper Fish Process
dance, abandonment in, 83
demonstration, explanation vs., 92–93
De Niro, Robert, 77
Duncan, Isadora, on explaining dance, 83

Eastwood, Clint, 72–73
editing film
as analogy to manager's task, 121–123
in film industry, 93, 116–118
efficiency, administrative, 66
Einstein, Albert, on imagination, 55–56
emotions, in letting go of creation, 55
employees
creativity in, 59
time for, during autonomy stage, 74–76
exchange, 91–102
compassion in, 94

demonstration vs. explanation in, 92–93
givers and receivers in, 93–94
intimacy of, 91–92
manager's role in, 94–96
in *Maple* newspaper case, 96–102
explanation, demonstration vs., 92–93

facilitator, manager as, 111
failure, risk of, 115–116
fatigue, 111
filmmaking
by Woody Allen, 82–83
by Clint Eastwood, 72–73
editing in, 93, 116–118
by Thelma Schoonmaker, 93, 116–117
"first draft" of idea, 74
Ford, Henry, 118, 119
Friday morning idea-sharing, 67
functionality, competent, 65
future, imagining, 56

gas engines, 118
Gates, Bill, 56
generosity
of mind, 63
with "play," 64
givers, in exchange stage, 93–94
giving life to ideas, 63
global marketplace, uniqueness in, 65
Greenfield Village, 119
group creative projects
collaboration in, 106
exercise for, 86–87
letting go in, 83–84
Grove, Andy, 56

Home Theater Magazine, 93
honoring
of autonomy, 85
of creative process, 121
Hopkins, Anthony, 77
human body, collaboration in, 104–105
humility, 62

ideas
as "action-potentials," 64
adaptation of, 127
control of, 62
discovering merit of, 106

Index

Index

About the Author and Illustrator

Jonathon Flaum is CEO of WriteMind Communications, an Asheville, North Carolina–based consultancy focused on organizational creativity and public communication. Through speeches, seminars, and workshops, WriteMind facilitates opportunities for organizations to explore the creative process that leads to innovation. With regard to public communication, WriteMind works with corporate leaders to help them integrate their authentic personal voice with their business objectives when delivering a speech or presentation to their company or industry group or when writing an article for publication.

In addition to running WriteMind Communications, Jonathon serves as the chief editorial consultant for the

About the Author and Illustrator

Louisiana State University Neuroscience Center of Excellence. Jonathon is coauthor of the book *The 100-Mile Walk: A Father and Son on a Quest to Find the Essence of Leadership*, published in January 2006. He writes the weekly "Meaning at Work" column for the *Asheville Citizen-Times*. Jonathon holds a master of arts in philosophy of religion from Florida State University and a master of fine arts in playwriting from the University of Southern California.

WriteMind offers a variety of training courses, seminars, and interactive experiences in "Daishinji Management." For further information see www.paperfishprocess.com or www.writemindcommunications.com or contact Jonathon directly at Jonathon@writemindcommunications.com.

Raina Bays studied drawing and painting at the School of the Art Institute of Chicago and then focused on master oil techniques under the guidance of Joseph Biel in Portland, Oregon. She continues to work in oils as well as acrylic and charcoal and enjoys the vibrant arts and crafts community of her home in Asheville, North Carolina.